CLARENCE L. AND ESTELLE S. ...
Reform Congregation Keneseth Israel
Elkins Park, Pa. 19117

Between the Generations:
A Jewish Dialogue

Samuel H. Dresner has also written:

Prayer, Humility and Compassion
The Zaddik
Three Paths of Man and God
The Jewish Dietary Laws
God, Man and Atomic War
The Sabbath

Between the Generations: A Jewish Dialogue

By

SAMUEL H. DRESNER

HARTMORE HOUSE

To the next generation:

Hannah
Miriam
Nahama
Rachel

Copyright © 1971 by
Hartmore House, Inc.
An Affiliate of Media Judaica, Inc.
1363 Fairfield Avenue
Bridgeport, Connecticut

All rights reserved, including the right to reproduce this book, or any portions thereof, in any form, except for the inclusion of brief quotations in a review.

Library of Congress Catalog Card Number: 79-172413

Printed in the United States of America

TABLE OF CONTENTS

I.	*Our* Young People	7
II.	**Double Standards**	13
	1. As Americans	13
	2. As Jews	21
	3. To Be or Not To Be	29
III.	**Bridging the Past**	32
	1. The Gap	33
	2. Why a Gap?	43
	3. The Turning	49
IV.	**Judaism as Radical Revolution**	53
	1. Personal Life	60
	2. Economic Life	68
	3. Political Life	72
	4. The Underground	75

BETWEEN THE GENERATIONS

I

OUR YOUNG PEOPLE

College of Fine Arts,
Albany, N. Y.

Dear Mother and Dad:
  It has been three months since I left for college. I have been remiss in writing, and I am very sorry for my thoughtlessness in not having written before. I will bring you up to date now. But, before you read, please sit down. O.K.?
  Well then, I am getting along pretty well now. The skull fracture and the concussion I got when I jumped out of the window of my dormitory when it caught fire shortly after my arrival are pretty well healed now. I only spent two weeks in the hospital, and now I can see almost normally and get those sick headaches only once in a while.
  Fortunately, the fire in the dormitory and my jump were witnessed by an attendant at the gas station near the dorm, and he was the one who called the fire department and the ambulance. He also visited me at the hospital, and since I had nowhere to live because of the burned out dorm, he was kind enough to invite me to share his apartment with him. It is really a basement room, but it's

kind of cute. He is a very fine boy and we have fallen deeply in love and are planning to get married. We haven't set the date yet, but it will be before my pregnancy begins to show.

Yes, Mother and Dad, I am pregnant. I know how much you are looking forward to being grandparents, and I know you will welcome the baby and give it the same love and devotion and tender care that you gave me when I was a child. The reason for the delay in our marriage is that my boyfriend has some minor infection which prevents us from passing our premarital bloodtests, and I carelessly caught it from him. This will soon clear up with the penicillin injections I am now taking daily.

I know you will welcome him into our family with open arms. He is kind, and although not well-educated, he is ambitious. Although he is of a different race and religion than ours, I know your often expressed tolerance will not permit you to be bothered by these facts.

Now that I have brought you up to date, I want to tell you that there was no dormitory fire; I did not have a concussion or a skull fracture; I was not in the hospital; I am not pregnant; I am not engaged; I do not have syphillis; and there is no one in my life. However, I am getting a D in History and an F in Science, and I wanted you to see these marks in their proper perspective.

Your loving daughter,
Edna

On reading such a letter, we can hardly suppress a smile or even a laugh. Perhaps it is good that we are still able to laugh. Had we read it ten years ago, no doubt we would have roared. Our laughter today, however, has a hollow ring about it. It is, in fact, a "bittere gelechte." For though the letter concludes on a humorous note, implying that all along it was meant only as a farce, the calamities it catalogues are very real to parents who have either already experienced their share of tragedy or tremblingly anticipate it. To paraphrase the Egyptians' lament at the plague of the first-born, "There is hardly a home which has not suffered."

But if there are letters like the above which may reflect an immature, pleasure-seeking, spoiled generation of problem children, recklessly delighting in "liberating" themselves in ever more shocking ways from the mores of society, there are also other letters and pronouncements of a far more serious nature from individuals and student protest groups appearing in campus papers, national publications, and conferences, which reflect a widely growing disenchantment and a rejection of what they feel are the immoralities of our society.

Several years ago, for example, it was announced that for the first time in its history, Barnard, one of the exclusive Seven Sister Colleges, had canceled its senior prom. Explained the student chairman of the event: "Such parties aren't relevant. People don't want to get dressed up in pretty dresses and go off to the Plaza when children are starving in Biafra and there's a war in Vietnam." In place of their traditional Greek Games, held annually for sixty-six years, the girls also had a "more relevant" Spring Festival at which the students called upon the philosophy department to hold informal discussions with them and their parents about the campus revolution.

But regardless of whether we adopt George Kennan's dim view of the revolt of the young as "wallowing in drugs, pornography, and hysterical politics,"[1] or see it as an idealistic refusal to accept an immoral status quo, the irreducible fact of the matter is that these young people are, in large measure, *our* children. Estimates of the percentage of Jewish students involved in campus protests have gone as high as fifty percent, and one investigator calculated that about twenty-five percent of the hippies in Haight-Ashbury were Jewish. Only scan the names of campus heroes in any news report—Rubin, Rudd, Cohn-Bendit, Hoffman, Dohrn (Orenstein)—and it will be obvious that Jewish students are participating in an extraordinarily vital way in this upheaval which so agitates the college generation. Jews, then, have a special concern, whether they approve or not.

The problem of the relationship between the generations, or, as we prefer to name it today, the "generation gap," rages as perhaps the central issue for innumerable Jewish parents and for the Jewish community as a whole. "Generational conflict, generational struggle," remarks Lewis Feuer in his book *Conflict of Generations*, "has been a universal theme of history. Unlike class struggle, however, the struggle of the generations has been little studied and understood."[2] The tension between "fathers and sons" (to use Turgenev's phrase) finds no more illuminating analysis than the Book of Genesis itself, most of whose chapters deal with this very theme as it affects Abraham and his sons, Isaac and his sons, and Jacob and his. The words, "the two of them walked together," which resound again and again in the awesome testing of Abraham and Isaac, evoke the ideal picture of the generations.

Birth, the bringing of a child into the world, is surely

one of man's deepest mysteries, but a far greater enigma is what happens to that child as he matures and grows to manhood. Where will he stand then in relation to those parents who first brought him into the world and what will determine his stand? Will he accept and continue what they struggled for, or will he tear out the very roots from which he grew?

The present crisis of the generation gap reflects a growing chasm between parents and children—a chasm of misunderstanding, rebellion, rejection, frustration, and terrible anguish. To be sure, there is a good deal about the revolt of the young to annoy the older generation—shoulder-length hair, offensive language, and frequently foolish, and even destructive, tactics. But it would be tragic if we let our gaze stop there and failed to view the scene as a whole, appreciating the remarkable potential for the improvement of conditions which the present unrest contains. Indeed, as John D. Rockefeller II indicated in an article in the *Saturday Review*, "The crucial issue is not the revolt of youth but the nature of our response to it."[3] The article warns against two possible dangerous responses: "suppression"—which will only encourage the extremists—and "apathy"—which will only serve to delay matters, since the current youth revolt is no normal rebelliousness of the young that time will cure.

"The greater tragedy," continues Rockefeller, "will be the opportunity we will have lost. For we know all too well that time is running out on the great problems the world faces. It seems to me that we have a choice. By suppression or apathy, we can make the youth revolution into yet another problem—in which case the burden will become crushing. Or we can respond in positive ways so that the energy and idealism of youth can be a constructive force in helping to solve the world's great problems.

The third possible response, then, is simply to be responsive—to trust our young people, to listen to them, to understand them, to let them know we care deeply about them."

This book is an attempt to do just that.

By listening to the young and trying to understand the reasons for the generation gap which has emerged, we shall attempt to derive three lessons for the modern Jew, which, if taken to heart as a program for private living and community endeavor, may help to bridge that gap.

BETWEEN THE GENERATIONS

II

DOUBLE STANDARDS

1.

As Americans

The first lesson we have to learn is that we can *no longer tolerate the hypocrisy of double standards*! It is precisely this which characterizes so much of American and Jewish life, and which is at the very heart of what is being rejected by young people today.

Writing in the *New York Times Magazine*, novelist James Michener catalogued some of these double standards that infect our society: "We say we believe in nobility—but not for the blacks. We say we believe in the Christian ethic—but not in business. Across the country, we preach morality—but not in the country club. Unctiously, we stamp our letters, 'Pray for Peace'—but vilify anyone who works for it. We proclaim ourselves a non-violent people—but we insist that each man be allowed to have his own gun to blast down anyone with whom he disagrees. And our whole society, especially T.V., indoctrinates us with a creed of accumulation, and then we discover that this brings neither happiness nor stability."[4]

Michener's paradigm of perversity deserves a closer look. That the war in Vietnam is a vicious exercise in double standards, few will deny today. We insist on the principles of national self-determination and non-intervention, condemn wanton destruction of non-military targets, and counsel the use of force only as a final resort after all other efforts fail, while at the very same time we have repeatedly and excessively violated these principles over the last five years in Vietnam. In the minds of many Americans, including Congressmen and other leaders of the country, we are involved in an immoral war.

We label the Viet Cong conscienceless killers, and yet it is they and not we, who, upon gaining control of a territory, divide it among the people, hold elections, and establish a school committee as matters of first priority. We proclaim American moral superiority, yet venereal disease and heroin are doing as much harm to our soldiers as enemy guns. We have defended a corrupt government, manipulated its leaders, and tolerated unbelievable mishandling of American supplies. Instead of finding a moral solution to a political problem, many feel we are perpetrating mass murder. Symbolic of the absurdity of the entire undertaking is the observation of an American general: "We had to destroy this town in order to save it!"

Let us remember that the immorality of the Vietnam war is an issue which student protests first raised and kept at the boiling point until public opinion had been so aroused that a President of the United States was forced to withdraw his candidacy for reelection!

Twenty-five years ago the great Swedish sociologist, Gunnar Myrdal, laid the festering, but then manageable, Negro problem at the evil door of double standards. He called his book *An American Dilemma* to emphasize the fact that the crux of the issue was the continuing conflict between conscience and behavior, between what America said it was—a land of liberty and justice for all—and what it really was—the land of liberty and justice for all, except the Negro. The fraud which, for more than two hundred years, has been perpetrated upon the Negro and, no less, upon America itself, has been uncovered in all its ugliness. Instead of taking massive, immediate steps to eradicate this hypocrisy, we dawdled with half-hearted efforts during the years when Negroes were seeking integration and their leaders were non-violent. As a result, in the place of Christian non-violence, we have black racism, black militancy, black hatred, and the demand for black power, which is as vicious and as dangerous as anything one can find in the white community. I shudder to think what the coming decade holds in store for America in the way of race relations, the tragic rise in Negro anti-Semitism being only one byproduct of inaction and irresponsibility. We have sown the wind and reap the whirlwind!

Many young people feel that the problem of poverty—after cutting through all the verbiage, sweeping aside all the surveys, and reaching bedrock—is nothing more or less than the problem of hypocrisy. How is it possible, they ask, that in Sweden there is no poverty and in Denmark there are no slums, while in America, which contains a mere six percent of the world's population but sixty percent of its wealth, our cities are crumbling and people are deprived and hungry?

How, indeed, can one explain it, except as the young themselves do: (1) Despite legislation to alleviate poverty, the rich would seem to benefit more than the poor from our laws. For example, Alvin Schorr points out in his *Explorations in Social Policy*, that in 1962 the Federal contribution to low-cost housing for the bottom fifth of the population was $820 million, while the subsidy to the top fifth in the form of tax deductions was $1.7 billion.[5] To take a single case, in 1968 Senator James Eastland received more than $200,000 in government subsidies for his cotton plantation in Sunflower County, Mississippi. (2) Granting considerable progress, we have failed to carry out adequately the Biblical injunction that wealth implies responsibility, still preserving an antiquated quasi laissez-faire mentality, whose original function of providing incentive to the industrial revolution has been inoperative for a century and has instead contributed to the growing extremes of rich and poor. (3) Finally, we have bungled our sense of priorities in preferring to allocate the bulk of our material resources toward the cause of a morally questionable war abroad, whose cost in human life is staggering, instead of using it to wage the pressing moral battle at home to eradicate poverty, decay, and corruption.

Dr. D. A. Zoll of the University of Saskatchewan, Canada, once observed that our society has sought to tranquilize youth by dangling in front of it a collection of prizes to be won by good cooperative behavior. The prizes include: education, jobs, security, a glittering collection of rewards and a high standard of living.

But something has gone awry. Many young people are not behaving according to expectation. They have ceased cooperating. Prizes for which the past generation would have given almost anything no longer attract. Having grown up with them and observed them at first hand, the young find them wanting. "Education" is too often irrelevant; "jobs" are meaningless; "security" is seen as surrender, "rewards" as punishments, and "a high standard of living" as only a mask to hide the anguish that lies beneath the surface of our private, family, or business lives. The young are no longer willing to be seduced into such a world.

"It is quite right that the young should talk about us as hypocrites. We are," conceded Judge Charles E. Wyzanski, Jr. in an address at Lake Forest College. "And it is quite right that they should note that our hypocrisy is embedded in our materialism."[6]

Young people today are questioning the doctrine that production and consumption should continue to be, as they have been for generations past, the primary goals of American life. Born into a society where financial security no longer requires the bitter struggle it used to, and where one's basic needs are virtually guaranteed, they are, according to sociologist Amitai Etzioni, "much less interested in consuming goods and services and much more concerned with social justice."[7] They are expressing the philosophy which Galbraith enunciated so well in his book, *The Affluent Society*, which described America as a land of private affluence—our homes, cars, security—and public poverty—our schools, hospitals, etc. What this amounts to is a distorted sense of national priorities.

Consider the following figures.

Though we lead the world in per capita medical expenditures, medical research, and hospital service, we are sixteenth in infant mortality and twentieth in longevity.

Though we are the greatest builders of history, we have demolished more houses than we have built with Federal funds. We need 2,600,000 units per year, yet we build at the rate of 1,600,000 and tolerate 10,000,000 substandard houses.

Though we have the highest percentage of college students in the world and spend the most for education, 28 percent of our youth do not graduate from high school, 16 percent of those tested for military service in the past fifteen years have been rejected for educational deficiency, and the rate of high school dropouts in New York City is 37 percent; in Detroit, 38 percent; and in Philadelphia, 47 percent.

We spend fifty times as much on highways between cities as we do on those transit systems within cities on which the poor depend to reach work.

Though rising crime, which shocks the nation, costs 50 billion dollars a year, we spend only five billion on all means of crime prevention: law enforcement, prisons, etc. This is about the sum we spend on toilet articles.

The Office of Economic Opportunity (OEO) has a budget just two-thirds as high as what we spend on jewelry per year, or one-twelfth of what goes towards the purchase of tobacco and alcohol.

We spend almost ten times as much on pet food and care as we do on food for the poor.

Though we have had an unprecedented one hundred months of prosperity, twenty-two million Americans still live in poverty.

Though we have produced job opportunities for eight and one-half million people in the last five years, the same number is on welfare.

The violence which has at times broken out on college campuses, while not to be justified, may be explained in part by the deep frustration students feel at broken promises and hypocritical commitments, whether regarding Vietnam, the war on poverty, or the failure to redirect national priorities.

One of the clearest expressions of student feeling that has yet appeared was issued in a letter to President Nixon from Dr. Calvin Plimpton, president of Amherst College: "We believe that we must speak out to make clear that much of the turmoil among young people and among those who are dedicated to humane and reasoned changes will continue. It will continue until you and the other political leaders of our country address more effectively, massively, and persistently, the major social and foreign problems of our society. Part of this turmoil in universities derives from the distance separating the American dream from the American reality."[8]

A president of the National Student Association described his generation as the first "post-war, post-Depression, post-Bomb, post-space generation. It is also," adds Roderick MacLeish, "the first generation in modern history to move toward adulthood without having to worry about how to make a living ... They (sic) assume affluence is a permanent condition, not a goal to be achieved. Free of any necessity to struggle for economic security, the post-everything generation is highly imbued with man's restless quest for the perfection of his own condition, and has turned upon the imperfections of society."[9]

Young people have good reason to tell us to stop compromising and begin living as we know we ought to live. They are no longer satisfied with changes that come slowly through our maze of legislative and judicial systems. Changes take too long, they complain, and the young, in any case, do not have the power to bring them about. So they demand immediate change, press for a "participatory" democracy in which they have a say now, bypassing the slow motion of courts, Congress, and elections in favor of active protest, which occasionally erupts into riots. Had the slow process of government been moving in a clear, steady, responsible fashion to solve the nation's problems, the crisis of youth protest probably would not have come about. But with the realities of widespread political corruption, the interminable red tape of judicial delay, and power blocs of immense wealth lobbying effectively, they fear there may not be time to halt a society hurtling to disaster before the Bomb goes off—or before any one of a dozen equally devastating and more insidious natural disasters occur.

Since the end of World War II, we have been rearing Bomb-obsessed offspring: children unable to free their subconscious from the spectre of nuclear war. Their parents can try to retreat mentally to the security they once knew in the pre-atomic world; the children cannot.

A report given at the William Alanson White Institute of Psychiatry by two doctors who had studied the reactions of grade school children to atomic war, revealed that kindergarten teachers indicate a growing preoccupation of children with pictures of destruction. Grey mushroom clouds are replacing the sun and sky in their drawings. There is even a joke among ten year-olds: "What are you going to be *if* you grow up?" The children seem to understand quite well, the doctors tell us, that the present threat is different from all previous ones.[10]

Moreover, a new source of fatalism exists today, inspired by fears to which, until only recently, an advanced technological society was believed immune. Over-population, famine, disease, revolution, depletion and contamination of resources—alone or in combination, any of these natural disasters is suddenly as real a threat of devastation as the Bomb.

This generation's early awareness of the precariousness of its existence sheds new light on the alarming growth of teenage and college rebellion against accepted mores. It has its roots, largely, in attitudes of fright and despair acquired by growing up in a world where all the lessons of past generations, all the books, ideas, and standards which are their heritage appear useless, and even hypocritical, if there will be no future in which to apply them and no next generation to benefit from their experience. If this is the end, they argue, then what is the sense of it all?

Young people, says John Wharton, summing up their

despair, "see that the accepted and entrenched educational, economic, and political systems have produced a world with more warfare, bigger massacres, more powerful criminals, and more overall violence than at any other time since the Age of Enlightenment began. Yet many of the leaders of these systems are still spouting platitudes which, to the young people, are patent expressions of either ignorance, self-delusion, or pure hypocrisy. Moreover, not only do these older folk refuse to admit any incompetence; they actually boast of the eminence that they have achieved—utterly unaware that to youth *this* is proof of incompetence. When one is part of a system that has brought a whole world to disaster, only a fool boasts that he is an *important part*. Yet these are the people, say our youth, who have the unmitigated gall to expect that we will gladly accept them as fit to train us for *any* kind of leadership.

"Youth's first reaction to all of the foregoing is one of frustration, rage, and desire to destroy. The situation is similar to a man trying to learn to ride a bicycle with such crooked handlebars that he always finds himself in the ditch. He tries to fix it; he can't; no one helps him; in a rage he kicks the whole thing to pieces."[11]

2.

As Jews

Jewish college students do not halt with a critique of America. They see themselves as Jews as well as Americans and have a good deal to say on this score too.

Again and again I have heard the same kind of charges from the Jewish young people throughout the country with whom I have had an opportunity to speak.

We complain to them that their protests have turned into riots and violence.

And they answer: "What do you mean? What can you expect of us? Didn't you expose us as kids to thirty hours a week of violence and murder on TV, and didn't you give us a country where a president, a great civil rights leader, and a presidential candidate could all be assassinated without so much as a firm gun control law resulting? And didn't the momentary twinge you felt, that if one is guilty all are responsible, subside as you sat transfixed before those endless TV funeral spectaculars which drained the emotions, soothed the conscience, calmed the anguish, and served as a perfect substitute for the only thing that might help—actions! If you adults are casual about violence, what do you want from us?"

We object to some of their lax views on sex.

And they reply: "Did the hippies create *Playboy* magazine, the topless society, and the 'see-thru' dresses? Do they produce the pornographic novels, the Madison Avenue 'come-on,' the dirty-book stores, and the movies which publicize the homosexual and the pervert? Who gave the Communications Award to Hugh Hefner in 1964, young people or the Chicago Jewish Charities? And who paid the more than 2 million dollars that the brassiere industry reported was spent two years ago for bras for nine year old girls—the kids or their mothers?"

We berate them about drugs and point out the terrible dangers that they may cause.

But they say: "If we can have it documented that marijuana contributes to cancer, then can we get it legalized? If after all the medical findings, you are still smoking and permitting advertisements for smoking, then why bother us about our form of drugs? And if you drink liquor at meals, parties, and clubs, why deny us our kicks?

The only reason you pick on marijuana and not nicotine or alcohol is because there is big money behind them and enough of you are hung up on them and do not want to give them up!"

We ask why they are not closer to their parents and homes. And they shower us with complaints. Some claim they no longer have a home.

"Home," they say, "is a place to leave. It is a kind of dormitory, a place to eat and leave your coat. Everything takes place outside. You study in school, work in an office, are sick in a hospital, and are mourned in a funeral parlor. There isn't even much pressure any more from our parents to be home from college on Rosh Hashonah and Yom Kippur. So how important could home be for them? Of course, for some, distance and expense make it virtually impossible. But a lot of us could get home, if we thought it was really important. Do you know, Rabbi, what goes on at a college campus on Rosh Hashonah and Yom Kippur? Every year fewer students go home and more attend classes, even on the Day of Atonement. It has become pretty much of a school day, with a nod toward religion. Our parents know about it but don't seem to care. It's a kind of unspoken agreement. So what could home be anyway, if you spend the High Holidays on the college campus?"

Young people complain that the family is not what it was. "First of all," they object, "we move around too much, because it seems that in order for our fathers to move up economically, they have to move out. We don't like that. We're told that there was a time when the family was 'a family' with cousins and uncles and aunts. But now, for us, it has contracted into what sociologists call the 'nuclear family'—that is, father, mother, and children. And that is it! You don't care about the others; you don't see them or speak to them except at funerals and weddings. That's not much of a family, is it?"

Young people see the success mania decimating the home and often making them feel in the way and unwanted. "When our parents want to play golf, or go to Florida or to a cocktail party, what do they do with the kid? They give him the great electronic pacifier—television! Children are dependent upon the love and guidance of the parents. Instead, they get presents." Some college students say that the business world is destroying their fathers. "A child wants a father who is whole, complete, authentic," they explain. "But the economic battlefield seems to fragment a man: at the office he must restrain himself, depersonalize himself, delegate authority, get the best out of people, be tough and conscienceless in order to reach or remain at the top; while at home he is supposed to be loving, altruistic, and kind. It must be terribly hard, though, to turn on and turn off every day like a Jekyll and Hyde. And this takes its toll on all of us at home."

Perhaps more than anything else, however, young people are critical of religion. "The synagogue is designed to walk some very mediocre, middle-of-the-road line," one student observed. "It is not supposed to rock the boat or to make anybody feel." "Those non-alienating sermons," commented another student. "My rabbi sounded like a combination of *Readers Digest* and *Life Magazine*—and that can be a really depressing experience."

One of the reasons so many young people are turned off by religion is their parents' double standards. " 'You've got to go to synagogue, got to go to synagogue.' 'Yes, Mother, I know I've got to go to synagogue.' *She* doesn't go to synagogue and *she* is yelling at me, 'You can't do this, you can't do that, you can't go out with boys who aren't Jewish . . . ' "[12]

We ought to pay special attention to what young people have to say on the score of religion. Some of it may be wrong, but we should listen anyway, because much of it may be right. Youngsters are less impressed than their parents by the beautiful synagogue buildings that dot the landscape of suburbia. The 10 million dollar temple may move them less than a *shul* with ten members, all of whom keep the Sabbath. They want the answers to some very obvious but uncomfortable questions. Here are a few of them:

"What do you want a synagogue for anyway?"

"What are the priorities that you set in running the synagogue?"

"How much of the budget is going to social action, youth activities, education, adult education?"

"Even boy scouts must fulfill certain requirements to be accepted as members. Assuming that belonging to a synagogue is at least as important as belonging to Scouts, what is required of one to join, apart from having a Jewish mother and a checkbook?"

"What higher requirements are there for officers and board members of the congregation, sisterhood and men's club?"

"How much of the agenda for board meetings is devoted to the budget and how much to education and personal commitment?"

"How does the synagogue deal with a member who is a slumlord? Is the matter passed over in silence so long as he makes his financial contribution?"

"Why do you permit synagogue programs that have no Jewish purpose, such as sports heroes and comedians?"

"What is the synagogue doing to promote Sabbath observance?"

"Civil rights is a Jewish issue. What are the synagogues—

apart from their rabbis—doing about it? How can you explain that several summers ago, while 50 percent of the young volunteers who went south to Mississippi were Jewish, they received their orientation from the National Council of Churches?"

Such questions are not easy to answer. Further, young people claim there is a credibility gap between themselves and us. What kind of credibility gap? They do not believe that we believe!

I asked one youngster what this meant. "Why don't you believe that we believe?"

"Because," he replied, "most parents are 'neither/nor' Jews."

" 'Neither/nor!' What is that?" I asked.

"Well," he said, "let me explain it this way. You can play the 'neither/nor' game at the next cocktail party. Just go up to somebody and ask, 'Are you religious?' "

" 'No, of course not,' he will probably respond."

" 'Well,' you continue, 'you must be anti-religious then?' "

" 'Why no,' he will protest. 'How silly! I'm not against religion. It's quite nice to be religious.' "

"That's what I call a 'neither/nor' Jew."

"Or again, ask, 'Do you keep kosher?' "

" 'No, I don't keep kosher.' "

" 'Then you must be against keeping kosher?' "

" 'Certainly not. It's nice to keep kosher. Some of my best friends keep kosher. As a matter of fact, my own daughter-in-law has decided to keep kosher!' "

"What is he? He's 'neither/nor.' "

"Or ask someone, 'Do you go to synagogue on the Sabbath?' "

" 'No, I don't.' "

" 'Then you must be opposed to going to synagogue?' "

" 'How stupid! Naturally I am not opposed. Come to think of it, when I go on the High Holidays or for a bar mitzvah, I actually enjoy it.' "

" 'What is he? 'Neither/nor.' "

"Now, this is sheer unmitigated nonsense," young people continue. "Either you say yes or no. If you think that going to synagogue or keeping kosher is right, then go to synagogue and keep kosher, and if you don't think so, don't be afraid to say so. But the 'neither/nor' posture means quite simply that you take a frivolous view of the whole thing. How can you expect us then to believe that you believe?"

When the role of Judaism today is facetiously described as "hatch, match, and dispatch"—because it is, alas, only at birth, marriage, and death that it touches most people—we take it as a joke. But to the young people, it is no joke. It is a *betrayal*. To them God exists everywhere or nowhere; He is concerned with everything or nothing, relevant to our entire life or to none of it, supremely important or not important at all.

One of the most frustrating topics to raise with young people is intermarriage. I have had many such conversations with those who face real problems or who are just exploring future possibilities. But whether or not a mate is at hand, one will often hear this kind of argument:

"I don't understand my parents, rabbi. I have gone out with gentile girls since high school and nothing much was said then. True, some objections were raised at first, but when I pressed the issue, pointing out that these were my friends, that this was the American way, and besides, everybody else interdated, they could not give any good reasons why I shouldn't. Of course, they might have told me that all dating is preparation for marriage, and the best way to prevent intermarriage is not to interdate. And they would have been right. As a matter of fact, that is exactly how I fell in love with Pat. But then they would have had a harder problem to explain: why intermarriage itself is wrong. They couldn't do that then and can't now. Sure, they object, but it doesn't make sense to me. Take my Bar Mitzvah, for example. The whole thing was a farce, one big birthday party. All I heard around the house was invitations, menus, and gifts. Sure they dropped me off for services a few times, but I caught on pretty quickly that this was kid stuff, and when you grow up, you grow out of it. I stopped Hebrew school shortly afterwards without too much noise. Look, my parents don't practice Judaism. They don't know anything about it.

"Let me give you an example. We get two bulletins at home every week, one from the synagogue, the other from the country club. One announces a service on Friday night, the other a party; one is kosher, the other features lobster and bacon; one celebrates God; the other, money and the body. These are two conflicting, competing worlds. My parents belong to both. Which one has their loyalty? At school we are arguing about whether or not to become conscientious objectors and perhaps go to jail; at home they are debating whether or not to keep the club open on Rosh Hashanah. At school we are agitated about poverty and civil rights; at home the talk is all cars, golf, clothes, and business. At school we are afraid of the Bomb; at home they're afraid of the Department of Internal Revenue. I think my interests are more Jewish than theirs!

"And now they get all excited simply because I want to marry the girl I love. They got rid of their Jewishness despite marrying Jews; maybe I'll be more Jewish marrying a gentile. Their arguments are basically tribal arguments: be loyal to the tribe, what will people say ... Come to think of it, there is an argument that might convince me, probably the only argument that could. But they've never given it. I mean the example of their lives, the conviction that Judaism is something uniquely precious which gives such meaning to being a Jew that one would want to be loyal, not to the tribe, but to the faith."

Are young people only negative in their attitudes toward the Jewish community? Not at all. They have some clear ideas of what they would like to see. For some time I have believed that the latent energy of young people, if properly channeled, could go a long way to restructuring the American synagogue. It may be that the young do not realize the potential that they possess, the willingness of elders to listen, and the possibilities of rapid change taking place. We ought to delight in the fact that the present generation of young people is not content to sail along apathetically but has become concerned about present conditions. They can bring a new vigor to solving old problems and new vitality to present leadership.

Synagogue leaders should do what they can to encourage the young to submit their ideas. These might help to begin the renaissance we await and need.

3.

To Be or Not to Be

We have reached the end of an era in American Jewish history. For the past century we have stumbled along without breaking both feet, because an immigration, both massive and uninterrupted, provided ample numbers to fill immediately the ranks of those who were lost to us, so that their tragic desertion was hardly noticed. We could suffer Sabbathless homes, inadequate schools, standardless synagogues, and generally, a life of Jewish compromise during that long period of influx because they were not really essential to maintaining a community that could always draw new strength from the rich mixture of European Jews who were constantly reaching American shores.

This is no longer true. For a generation now, immigration has all but halted. More and more we are an American-born Jewish community, with the memories of Warsaw and Vilna, *yeshivas* and *kehillas*, students, scholars, and saints almost gone. Thus the two conflicting levels of what is expected of us as Jews and how we live as Jews can no longer be tolerated today. An American-spawned, American-educated, and American-motivated Jewish community is beginning to jell and we are confronted with the inescapable fact that it is by virtue of our own institutions, homes, and schools, their excellence, authenticity, and influence, that we shall rise or fall. Young people do not like what they see and they have no memories—not even at second-hand from parents—of what was. Nostalgia is no more. They judge Judaism not by Warsaw or Frankfurt but by Los Angeles and Chicago, by their own synagogue, Hebrew school, home, center, and club. To them, Judaism is either a serious demand on their lives or burdensome baggage to be dispensed with at the first opportunity.

Double standards may have worked for us once. Because we could depend on nostalgic memories and European immigration, we could close our eyes and get away with it.

Well, it will work no longer. That is what we are being told loudly and clearly by a generation without memories and, thanks to Hitler, without—ever again—East European immigrants.

We ignore that voice at the peril of our family lives.

Our children are demanding a showdown. They are asking us, once and for all, to decide whether we want to be Jews.

The choice is ours.

We may decide that we do not want to be Jews. Down through the ages there have always been some who, for whatever reason, have chosen to opt out. We have a perfect right to do the same. But then we must be ready to accept the inevitable consequences, certainly regarding our children.

Or we may decide we want to be Jews. If we do, we must understand something of what that means. It cannot be a casual approval. It must be taken seriously. It must affect our way of thinking and our way of living. There are certain demands which a great and holy tradition lays upon us—in our homes, in our business practices, in our daily actions, in our charity, and in the manner in which we treat our husbands or wives and raise our children.

Whoever thinks it is easy to raise a Jewish child is a fool. It takes unusual dedication to a constant goal, the willingness to sacrifice endlessly, and the courage to be a real person. Today young Jews are running to Indian mystics called gurus. Why? Because they are looking for significant models for their lives. And that is precisely what parents ought to be and what parents can be. But not enough parents have been. For a parent is a teacher—the first teacher. Even the schoolmaster, according to Jewish tradition, is only acting on the parent's behalf. During the early years of his life, it is the parent whom the child observes and is nurtured by, in the precious values of inner discipline, moral discrimination, endless hope, and hourly sanctification. These are the values which the spirit of Judaism has successfully handed down from generation to generation ever since God said of the first Jew, Abraham,

> "I have loved him, that he might command his children after him to keep the way of the Lord by doing justice and righteousness." (Gen. 18:19)

BETWEEN THE GENERATIONS

III

BRIDGING THE PAST

Why are there double standards in the first place? How did we get into a situation where hypocrisy has become so much a part of our lives? And where did the generation gap come from? Answers to such questions are not obvious. They have to be searched for.

Two of the most frequent reactions to the revolt of the young are to blame youth as irresponsible, spoiled, and immature; or to blame society for creating conditions—war, poverty, corruption, materialism—so intolerable as to force rebellion. The first has eyes only for the failures of youth, the second only for those of society. Surely there is some truth to both. Could there, however, be a further reason, namely, that the plight of the young goes back to the plight of their parents?

Could there, in fact, be two generation gaps, one between parents and children, and the other between parents and grandparents? And could not that gap between the present and the future have its origins, at least in part, in the one between the present and the past?

Young people reject the status quo for numerous reasons, some foolish, some serious. What are the serious ones?—the Vietnam War, the Atom Bomb, poverty amidst unequalled affluence, religious hypocrisy, and political and financial scandal so widespread that its shame rarely shocks any more. The young identify the status quo with us, the parent generation, and the institutions we maintain —the so-called Jewish "establishment"—including the synagogue. Since, they claim, we support and are a part of the status quo, we deserve to be rejected along with it.

Consider the matter. If it is in fact true that the Jewish community associates itself with an immoral and hypocritical society, does it not deserve to be rejected not only by the young, but by Heaven as well? Can such a community still claim the name Jewish? There is good reason to doubt that the teachings of Judaism which prevailed in the past are compatible with prevalent societal values which we accept today. In fact, there is a serious breach between us and our past. Bridging this gap to the past is the first step to removing the present generation gap.

1.

The Gap

How do we go about repairing the gap with the past? There are several steps. *First, we must admit that there is a gap.* The sick man cannot recover his health without first confessing his illness.

Naturally, we do not like to make confessions. We cannot deny that there are vast differences between ourselves and previous generations, but we tend to reduce them to externalities such as language, manner of dress, and social behavior. But what about that central core of unique qualities which has always endured in the past and which we tend to assume continues to endure in us? We like to believe that the kind of Jewish life we lead today—our centers, community councils, federations and synagogues—is a harmonious continuation of what always was, that our present Jewish life style simply extends, in a different garb, language, and land, what has ever been before, that contemporary Judaism is authentic and normative.

The underlying theme of some Jewish writers is likewise continuity with the past. Instead of asserting, however, that Jewish life is as noble now as it was then, their point is the reverse: it was just as rotten then as it is now! They attempt to prove this by dwelling on the shortcomings of East European Jewish life and ignoring its glory. One might think, from reading them, that Polish Jewry consisted of nothing but brothels, bandits, and witchcraft. The distortions which their own Jewish insecurity calls forth are obvious to anyone at all familiar with the facts.

Only compare the parody on the rabbinate which appears in *Fiddler on the Roof* with the way Sholem Aleichem himself, who made fun of everything but religion, treated the subject; or the thesaurus of vulgarisms which Leo Rosten calls *The Joys of Yiddish* with the earthy holiness of the authentic tongue; or the demonic sex adventures that Bashevis Singer transmigrates from Chicago to Warsaw with the simple honest life as reflected in the Yiddish dailies of the latter city; or the crude tales of immigrant life that irresponsible, ignorant, and greedy young Jewish writers punctuate with four-letter English words translated into Yiddish, with Mendele's, not to speak of Heschel's, picture of old world Jewry. As Sylvia Rothschild has pointed out, instead of Jewish writers portraying the "edelkeit" and "menschlichkeit" of the Jewish mother,[13] we are blessed with Philip Roth's "complaint," Malamud's tempters and humiliaters, and Bruce Jay Friedman's new swinging mother who goes off to college with her son.

What such writers are saying is something like this:

"True, Jewish life is vulgar now, but it has always been vulgar. We don't have anything to be ashamed of. We aren't any different now than they were then."

Of course, it is much easier that way. If it was always like it is now, then we are not so bad after all. No need to beat our breasts and confess our inadequacies. Just deflate the past, demythologize the heroes of yore—the mother, the Yeshiva student, the rabbi, even the Yiddish language— and you make it much simpler for all of us today. Because if what so many authors of so-called Jewish fiction are saying is *not* true, if their tales are distortions which they have conjured out of ignorance, ambition, or self-hatred, if it really was only one-tenth as holy and chaste and humble and merciful and beautiful as some say, then we should break our bones rather than live as we do.

Consider only one fact. It took two centuries—from 1650 to 1850—for the Jews of New York to settle the first rabbi there! Imagine, a Jewish community enduring for two hundred years without a rabbi! To have lived without a roof over their heads, without bread, without shoes—all this would have been conceivable, for it happened innumerable times in the history of our people—but to be without a rabbi, without the treasure-house of Torah, of life, the only life worth living—incredible! It is a fact unusual in Jewish history, except for the tiniest settlements. And even there every conceivable sacrifice was made for the sake of Torah. I recently came across a reference to a Jewish community of two hundred families in Eastern Europe in the last century which employed six teachers and a shochet (ritual slaughterer)! Note, then, what that single fact about New York implies about the manner of Jews—vagabonds, ignoramuses, ne'er-do-wells in high proportion—who forsook the old country for the new, until Hitler's holocaust sent us waves of scholars and leaders as well. If America was admired as the "goldene medinah" (golden land), it was also feared as the "trefe medinah." Those who came had to be willing to sacrifice the one for the other. Only in such an environment could the radical Reform Judaism of an Isaac M. Wise or a David Einhorn, that could make no headway even in enlightened Germany, strike roots and become the dominant trend. Leaderless, there emerged painfully and clumsily the American Jewish community we know today. Dare such a community claim an unbroken continuity with the spiritual heritage of the past?

The incontrovertible fact is that there is a yawning chasm between this experiment, called the American Jew, and the normative Jew of past generations and other lands. That is why Abraham J. Heschel can assert today that "Judaism is the least known religion."[14] That sentence has never left my mind since the first time I heard it from his lips. Authentic Judaism, Heschel is saying, is not necessarily captured by Jewish institutions or Jewish life today; and if you want to discover it, you might make a mistake by reading novels about Jews, attending Jewish meetings, visiting Jewish schools, or even by going to the synagogue. That is why experiences such as Camp Ramah and trips to Israel must be made available to young people, to enable them to touch the bedrock of Jewish authenticity.

What kind of gap exists between the present and the past?

Certainly there is a gap in Jewish knowledge. In generations gone by, and not so far back, the rabbi was simply an adornment of learning to an already erudite community, for what Eastern European village did not boast of a minyan who were his equals, or almost his equals, in Torah. Early morning before work, late evening after work—for each man, all or part of the day was given to study. No one was exempt—neither rich nor poor. The YIVO Library of New York possesses a book with the stamp, "Society for the study of Mishnah of the woodchoppers of Berditchev." That immensely impressive, humble stamp tells more than all the learned sociological treatises. If there is not a gap in respect to Torah knowledge, then there is not a gap at all. Today, ignorance of our literature and our tradition is so rampant that the rabbi has become the sole repository of all wisdom and the reference source for the simplest of facts, from how to name a baby to whether shivah is seven days, three, or just one.

The gap in Jewish understanding is equalled by that in Jewish living. Then, there was the beauty of the Sabbath that brought rest and renewal one day in seven; the warmth of the Jewish home where the rhythm of the ceremonial year was marked by food, song, and prayer; even the "gass", the Jewish street, had its own special flavor. In those days a "Shabbos Jew" was a term of reprobation, applied to the Jew who attended the synagogue only on the Sabbath. Today, many Jews have great difficulty in simply knowing how to put on *tefilin* or follow the *siddur*—among the most elementary forms of Jewish observance—and a Jew who goes to *shul* occasionally on Sabbath receives the highest praise.

You may argue, of course, that the essence of the matter is not what one knows or even what one observes, but rather what one is; that being a Jew is more a matter of quality than quantity, of attitudes and inner feelings, and in these areas there has been no change. Thus, if we are good human beings, "Jews at heart," we say, we are in fact at one with our forefathers, even though we may have discarded a great deal of extraneous paraphernalia.

A Jewish heart! We claim that marvelous organ so easily. Do we know what it means? The *rachmones*, the sensitivity, the tears, the aches, the pain for others' suffering, the sharing of one's bread and bed, the intolerance of cruelty even to animals, the fear of evil, the scandal of cruelty, the love of God, the humbleness of soul, the modesty of manner. A Jewish heart! We utter the words so matter-of-factly, and with such sober certainty, one would imagine it could be had through a surgeon's transplant. No, space-age Jewry has no more claim on a Jewish heart than it does on Jewish knowledge or observance. I am not expressing a perverse private theory. Statistics can prove it. In Vilna one hundred years ago, where one third of the population was Jewish, the Jews numbered less than one percent of the criminals, murderers, rapists, drunkards, or unmarried mothers. The study of Torah and the fulfilling of the *mitzvot*—Jewish knowledge and Jewish living—served to insulate our people against the pagan values surrounding them, enabling them to maintain a fortress of holiness amidst moral oblivion.

Today, those who protect the walls of inner understanding and outer practice have fallen, opening the flood gates to the alien standards outside. And we have been inundated. The search for success at any price, the conviction that whatever brings pleasure is good—without exception—has created a veritable revolution in the Jewish soul. Jewish criminals abound; Jewish alcoholics are on the rise; and a higher percentage of Jews than the rest of the population are drug addicts. The rate of divorce, intermarriage, and illegitimacy among Jews has grown astronomically. The filth on newstands, in novels and movies is, in good measure, due to Jews. The three classic cases on pornography before the Supreme Court were: The Government versus Ralph Ginzburg, the Government versus

Shackman, and the Government versus Roth. The names speak volumes! Let us cease deluding ourselves in claiming a Jewish heart. It has, alas, changed, along with our understanding and living.

In generations past, the *kehillah* (Jewish community), was founded upon and functioned on the basis of Torah.

Today, our Jewish Federations and Community Councils are in the hands of professional "managers," whose activities are primarily fund-raising and whose highest goals are seldom the advancement of Torah.

In generations past, Judaism fashioned people. Out of a mass of protoplasm, whims, and notions, through an infinitely patient system of learning and living, a Jew—the most civilized creature man has yet produced—was created.

Now, we fashion Judaism to our own convenience, picking and choosing at will. If there is no good program on T.V., no bridge game to go to, and nothing doing at the club, then we *might* go to the synagogue Friday night. But that is for us to decide. How many close their stores and offices even on Rosh Hashanah? Ninety-five percent of the Jews in American say they believe in God, but eighty-three percent do not think such a belief has anything to do with their business practices or their political views!

We affiliate without affirming. We belong without bothering to consider what belonging means. We have organizations galore; we are joiners and we pay dues. But where is our commitment to what we join? And how Jewish, therefore, are most of those organizations? "Our synagogues are beautiful," writes Abraham Heschel, "but our homes are a wilderness. The true goal includes not simply joining the synagogue, but becoming a Jew! And that is a life-long process."[15]

In generations past, there was a "total" Judaism, which was as natural a part of the entire life of man as breathing or working. Not only the East European Jew felt this, but also those who lived in times and places closer in spirit to our own. So, in the fifteenth century, Abarbanel could, at the same time, be the treasurer of Spain and write a classical Hebrew commentary to the books of *Samuel* and *Kings*. Would that have been conceivable for a Baruch or a Morgenthau? The total Judaism of the past prevailed in ghetto or palace, amidst poverty and wealth alike.

Today, so much of what we see is "instant" Judaism. A derogatory ad appeared in the *New York Times* a few years ago,[16] picturing a can about the size of a baked bean tin which allegedly contained everything anyone could need to become Jewish. It was withdrawn because of complaints.

> INSTANT JUDAISM – – – – TWO FOR $2.00
>
> Contents: powdered chicken soup, instructions on holding a plush bar mitzvah at a Chinese restaurant, a note of introduction to Mr. Arthur Goldberg, a Cadillac registration, a guide to New York delicatessens, a list of local wholesalers, an application to a country club.
>
> Directions: Add soda water and stir.

In generations past, Jews knew who they were, what was asked of them, and where they were going. We are sure of none of these things today. Then, it was the law of God that was holy; life's struggle consisted of subduing man's will to the divine will. Today, power and pleasure are the twin idols we worship, and the struggle is more one of imposing man's will upon his fellows. The modern Jew may be more antiseptic and aesthetic than his ancestor, but how moral has he remained? For some, the gap has grown so large that one wonders if they have not ceased being Jews in any way but biologically. The Marranos assimilated outwardly, while remaining loyal inwardly. Has the modern Jew become a paradigm in reverse?

A piece of remarkable evidence from a social scientist illustrates the gap between the Jew of yesterday and his counterpart today and documents the willingness of the latter to accept contemporary American values which the former would have rejected. In his study of the Hasidim of Brooklyn (based largely on tape recorded remarks), Professor Jerome Mintz of the Folklore Institute of Indiana University observed the reactions of a group of pious European Jews transferred to America. The following sample, in broken English, records the reactions of a simple, devoted Hasid to the new world.

"Even though we live in America here very peacefully, we still feel very uncomfortable in this country. We feel the freedom and we appreciate the freedom very much. But the freedom is very hard on us. The way of making a living is very difficult for the way of life we want to lead. We religious Jews used to go pray every morning, every *mincha-ma'ariv*. It's impossible to pray *mincha-ma'ariv*. By the time you come from work on the train, it's over. So you have to pray by yourself. In the morning it's the same thing. You have to rush. Time is so short. Until you go shopping and this and that, you can't get to pray. You haven't got time to meet friends. Not meeting friends, and not learning with each other—it's hurting our belief; it's hurting our customs. There is a great deal of freedom. But our way of life, we believe, should not be tied to a materialistic way of life. And here, from the morning till night you always have to think about the dollar. Even to make a decent living you are tied twelve hours a day. A normal worker, without a college education, without some special trade, he doesn't make more than $1.50 hour. And our families, and we believe in bigger families, our families have six or seven kids. And Jewish life is more expensive. Food is expensive, school is expensive, the holidays are more expensive. Even living very poor, we have to work twelve hours a day. And this hurts our way of life. Because for two or three years you work so hard you don't learn, you don't pray you fall back six years. You forget, and this is very bad. You have to continue to work spiritually. You can't work only when you're young and it keeps you your whole life. Man is never standing on the same point. Every day he is going up, or he's going down. He's always getting better or he's getting worse. This means that this way of life is very hard on us. We need an hour, two hours a day, a little freedom for our spiritual lives. You haven't got time to do mitzvahs, to do good deeds for each other. Before the war everybody had an hour or two to go for some poor people, to help some people at the hospital. Everybody had his own way. One hour a day to do good deeds. For us it is impossible. The way of life is so tense. Until you do something, the day is over.

"We still feel not free. Our minds are not free. You see, I can't put my mind to work whenever I want to. I like to learn, to study a little bit *Gemorah*, to talk to a friend of mine, to do a good deed. I can't because I have to be here in the shop to make a dollar. But I need the dollar. Not to buy myself a car. A dollar to buy bread and butter and milk, which in our way of life costs more than normal. Normal people who haven't got so much will say to their children, 'go in bad shoes.' No normal father of children can say, 'don't eat butter.' Here in America people should eat only bread and water? In Europe if the people don't eat butter, it's okay. Here, in America, in this country you shouldn't eat butter? You shouldn't eat meat at least three times a week? And there are people among us who don't eat because they can't afford it. Comes Passover, matzos are very expensive. Comes Sukkos, the sukkeh is expensive. You have to support the yeshivahs. We feel our children's lives depend on the yeshivah and you have to help them. If you pay twenty dollars for each child, you have four or five children in the yeshivah, it's quite a lot. It costs me a hundred dollars a month for the Yeshivah alone—besides supplies. You have to give charity also. You can't refuse anybody. You're a normal human being. You want to give, you have to give, you like to give. And the way of life is not set up for these expenses. Usually a worker who has a trade, he makes $2.00 an hour to $10.00. So he has for his food, for A & P, and schooling is free. So they have enough. He could even buy a car. He could even go out whenever he wants to. He doesn't have to learn. It doesn't bother him, if he stays an hour longer in the shop. Just the opposite. He's happy to be there an hour later. He feels that he does something worthwhile, he creates something, he makes another dollar. For us this is not creating, it's hindering. This is a very big point.

"We know there's more freedom in America than any place in the world. We don't complain about the freedom. But still, for our way of life, our type of people, we are not set up for this kind of life. Maybe other people are also unhappy. They don't know what's missing. But we, we felt already a different, a better way of life. So we know it's not right for us."[17]

2.

Why a Gap?

To admit that there is a gap between the present and the past is one step. The next is to endeavor to learn what its causes were, how it came about.

The reasons for the gap between the present and the past are much easier to understand than those for the present abyss. The former gap was between two continents, two languages, two styles of life, two universes of discourse. The world of the immigrant Russian Jews emerging from poverty and provincialism was rejected by their children who were striving to become Americanized. Everything they learned at the public school or saw on the street or hoped for in America seemed to be contradicted by their Old World parents who, unable to adjust, would have to pass away, as the Hebrew slaves did in the wilderness, so that the next generation might inherit the "promised land."

Lincoln Steffens, the master painter of American life, who was closely drawn to the Jewish immigrants of the East Side, describes the agony of the generations in his famous *Autobiography:*

"The tales of the New York ghetto were heart-breaking comedies of the tragic conflict between the old and the new. The very old, and the very new; in many matters, all at once; religion, class, clothes and manners, customs, language, culture. We all know the difference between youth and age, but our experience is between two generations. Among the Russian and other Eastern Jewish families in New York it was an abyss of many generations; it was between parents out of the Middle Ages, sometimes out of the Old Testament days hundreds of years B.C., and the children of the streets of New York today. We saw it everywhere all the time. Responding to a reported suicide, we would pass a synagogue where a score or more of boys were sitting hatless in their old clothes, smoking cigarettes on the steps outside, and their fathers, all dressed in black, with their high hats, uncut beards, and temple curls, were going into the synagogues, tearing their hair and rending their garments. The reporters stopped to laugh; and it was comic; the old men, in their thrift, tore the lapels of their coats very carefully, a very little, but they wept tears, real tears. It was a revolution. Their sons were rebels against the law of Moses; they were lost souls, lost to God, the family, and to Israel of old. Police did not understand or sympathize. If there was a fight—and sometimes the fathers did lay hands on their sons, and the tough boys did biff their fathers in the eye; which brought out all the horrified elders of the whole neighborhood and all the sullen youth—when there was a 'riot call' the police would rush in and club now the boys, now the parents, and now, in their Irish exasperation, both sides, bloodily and in vain. I used to feel that the blood did not hurt, but the tears did, the weeping and gnashing of teeth of the old Jews who were doomed and knew it. Two, three thousand years of continuous devotion, courage, and suffering for a cause lost in a generation?"[18]

The hardest blow for today's parents to accept is this: they believed that by breaking with their immigrant forbears they would be able to avoid a generation gap with their own children. Instead, they seem only to have succeeded in creating a wider gap. This comes as a shocking realization. All the sacrifice, all the adaptation for nothing! How did it happen?

Many of today's parents gave up the old ways—not only externals such as the Yiddish language, foreign dress, and bearded faces, but often essentials such as the Sabbath, kashrut, prayer, and Torah study—in order to take on those new ways which they thought spelled "American."

How much more American can you get than today's suburban Jewish parent: the mother, slim, well-dressed, plays golf and bridge and is up on the latest novels; the husband, one of the boys at the club, can mix drinks with the best and is not afraid of an off-color joke. These modern, up-to-date parents, were confident that their children, freed from old-fashioned "hang-ups" and raised according to the most permissive theories—"we'll give them everything we didn't have"—would be close to them in every way. The old division between the world of European parents and that of American-born children, which had given rise to so much anguish, misunderstanding, and rebellion, would be replaced by parents and children who were both American-born, English-speaking, hot dog-eating, baseball-playing, fun-loving creatures. Was it possible that children raised on Spock and given dancing lessons at eleven, would, despite it all, be alienated from their parents? After all, their own painful tranformation was only for the sake of their children!

However, the distressing truth is that parents who tried so hard to be modern, in order to be at one with their children, are now suffering from an alienation at least as severe as the one between themselves and their own parents.

Why?

Could it be because they are too modern and not authentic enough? Because they have given their children everything except what their children needed most—the knowledge of who they are? Becoming "American" was a consuming goal of the parents' lives. But their children, having been born in America, take their "American-ness" for granted. What perplexes them is their Jewishness.

Even as young children, they already know that an American is defined by religion, as either Catholic, Protestant or Jewish. They see Patty O'Connor going to parochial school, and Jimmy Nelson's family going to church, but they don't see their parents doing anything comparable, and they are confused. As they grow up and do not find religion in their own home, some have turned to substitute faiths. Perhaps part of the rebellion is the attempt of the young to discover their own identity.

Writing *In Defense of the Jewish Mother* Sylvia Rothschild tells us that "the Jewish mother and the modern woman have been at war for more than a hundred years. The Jewish mother's concern for an exemplary family and the perpetuation of her religion gave her life a less self-centered focus than her modern sister, more caught up with the future and the past. This was supplanted by the modern woman who was free to do as she pleased and could ignore religious laws, become self-centered and individualistic. In time the ideal of the Jewish mother was lost, misrepresented in fiction, and laughed at."

Mrs. Rothschild continues: "What is truly ironic is that the rebellion may be against the mothers who are not Jewish enough, who do not offer enough protection in early childhood, who do not help children to maturity and responsibility, who do not value adulthood and the lessons of the past."[19]

To understand better the dilemma of the gap between present and past generations, let us turn back to the classic source in early nineteenth century France.

Napoleon was one of the first who broke down the dark ghetto walls behind which European Jewry had been condemned to centuries of isolation, and allowed the Jews to emerge into what appeared to be the incredible splendor of the European nations. To enable them to adjust to the new conditions, Napoleon called together a Sanhedrin, the first that had been assembled for eighteen hundred years and one which he expected would do his bidding in emancipating Israel. In essence what he said to them was this: "To Jews as Frenchmen, I give everything; to Jews as Jews, I give nothing." This was to be the price for demolishing the ghetto and achieving freedom— to stop being a Jew!

For many of the Jews, to whom Judaism was either a meaningless collection of out-moded customs, a great religion of the past superseded by the new age of science, or simply an obstacle to the universal world that beckoned, the price was cheap. And they paid happily. Abandoning their faith, many eagerly drank in the prevailing myths of the nineteenth century: God was a hypothesis no longer needed; all mysteries would yield to human reason; religion was to be replaced by science, with the scientist playing priest; there was no chosen people, only men; and man himself had become God. "Glory to man in the highest," wrote Swinburne, "the maker and master of things."

So began the mass assimilation of the emancipated Jews in the decades that followed. Thousands did not hesitate to convert, more out of convenience than conviction; other thousands accepted radical social movements as the new religions that would save the world; still others remained Jews, but created a kind of attenuated caricature of Judaism which pruned it of its distinctiveness, permitted all things, and became little more than a "Mosaic Persuasion." The old cry, "Let us be like all the nations!" was heard once again in the frenzied drive for normalization. And once more Heaven responded; "They have abandoned Me!"

Then came the fateful day when truths held as sacred dogma in the nineteenth century were revealed as bitter illusions in the twentieth. We learned that human reason alone was frail, creating more mysteries than it solved; that science alone could produce an atom bomb but not tell you whether to use it for good or evil; that despite denials of chosenness, the world refused to cease singling out Israel for some special role, always placing it at the heart of every conflict or dream in the East and the West, in war and peace, the object of scorn and the glory of nations. The same Herzl, who but a few years before had hoped to solve the Jewish problem by proposing to the Pope a single mass conversion of Jews to Catholicism, experienced this sense of Israel's "chosenness" at the infamous Dreyfus trial in such a manner that his remaining years were totally transformed. Perhaps the most gifted assimilationist of them all was Heinrich Heine, who converted to Christianity as a passport to world acclaim and devoted his whole life to praising the superiority of the Greeks over the moralistic Hebrews, for their joy in beauty and sensual pleasure. Heine wrote on his death bed: "I see now that the Greeks were only handsome youths, while the Jews are always men, powerful, indomitable men, not only then, but to this very day."

Auschwitz and Hiroshima were the final convulsions that signaled the demise of all that had been hoped for. They shattered the last bastions behind which the nineteenth century myths had barricaded themselves. They also marked the end of the strange experiment called the modern Jew—one who cut himself off from his past roots, while still attempting to retain his present identity. Without the sap from the roots, the leaves withered, and the trees bore no fruit. The voice may have been the voice of Jacob, but the hands were the hands of Esau.

The experiment had failed.

3.

The Turning

What we see today is the emergence of a new kind of Jew, one who might best be called the "post-modern" Jew. This post-modern Jew will have had little difficulty in following the logic of the argument contained in these pages. It only confirms what he already knows. He is aware that the castle of the new age has collapsed because its foundations were set in shifting sands. The secular hope of life without God, which many Jews nurtured, has turned to ashes.

This post-modern Jew, with whom most of us can identify, is curious to learn who he really is—the history, hopes, and heritage of his tradition. Perhaps the most descriptive word for his present state of mind is a Hebrew one, a venerable one at that, with many overtones—*teshuvah*. It means to turn back, recapture, renew. We do not speak of a return to a segregated society, a special form of dress or language, but rather to a way of thinking and living—a Jewish way of thinking that will enable us to apply the wisdom of our heritage to the dilemmas of our time, and which will open up new dimensions of holiness in our homes and in our society.

Strange to say, one of the ways of bridging the gap to the past is by getting rid of our prejudices. There is, for example, a common prejudice against the Sabbath: the conviction that it cannot be observed in America. But there was never a country where it is easier to observe the Sabbath. The obstacles of a six-day economy and the sheer financial necessity of earning a bit more by working on the Sabbath are no longer severe obstacles. The growing five-day week and the mounting affluence have seen to that. But observance of the Sabbath should not be merely a question of convenience. No other single aspect of Judaism holds as much blessing for us, by binding families together, by teaching us to withdraw from the world of commerce, so that we turn away from the cares of the world for a day and open our hearts to God. We need to look at the Sabbath with objective eyes, to test it, to try it, to smell it, to allow its mood to envelop us so that we can savor the joy and wonder it holds in store.

We need to rid ourselves of the prejudice against keeping kosher, by dismissing those silly notions that kosher laws are health laws. Keeping kosher has to do with "being a Jew." It has to do with learning the lesson of reverence for life by removing the blood from an animal before we eat it, and by limiting the kind of animals we eat, turning the common act of eating into a moment when the goodness of God is recalled.

We need to remember that with the destruction of the Temple, each home was to become a miniature sanctuary, each table an altar, and each Jew a priest, ministering to the Almighty, in the holiness of his home with wife and children at his side.

We need to know that the Jew is called upon to be a witness to God, never fearing to speak the truth, to condemn evil, or to set his hand against injustice, no matter what the cost or how trifling the issue.

We need to recapture the sense of Israel's chosenness. There is such a thing as Jewish fate and Jewish faith. Judaism may have allies, even partners, but it has no substitute. What would happen to this world, God forbid, if Judaism disappeared? To have Judaism, you must have Jews—Jewish bodies in which there are Jewish minds and souls.

We need to be authentic Jews, Jews who allow the thunder of the prophets, the stillness of the Psalms, the wisdom of Moses, and the guidance of Akiba to enter their lives. A demand is made on us as Jews: something noble is expected. The program of the synagogue should express that demand, interpret that expectation, and give beauty, meaning and insight to our lives.

For if God is eternal, then the Torah, His teaching, and Israel, His people, are eternal. It is this eternity which unites the past, the present, and the future. We may not understand why, but it is so nonetheless. When we are at one with the past, so that Judaism becomes a living faith to us day by day, and Sabbath by Sabbath, then we can discover the hidden power we possess to transmit it to the next generation. When the Sabbath is sanctified, a blessing is said at the table, the Torah is studied, and the prophets' cry for justice resounds in our hearts, then we can become the bridge from the past to the future. For this is what Jewish parents are: the *bridge* between the past and the future.

The key to closing the generation gap to the future is first to close the gap to the past.

We parents may be the missing link!

BETWEEN THE GENERATIONS

IV

JUDAISM AS RADICAL REVOLUTION

Thus far we have derived two lessons from the generation gap.

The first was that we can no longer tolerate the hypocritical double standards that so many live by.

The second, emerging from our attempt to understand why hypocrisy has set such a deep mark on our lives, was that the new generation gap between parents and children may in some measure be explained by the older one between parents and grandparents, and that in order to bridge the gap between the present and the future, we should first close the one between the present and the past.

Now we come to the third and perhaps the most important lesson: *to win young people to Judaism, it is vital that we rid it of distortion and reveal its authentic form as the most radical revolution the world has ever known.*

If until now my remarks have been directed primarily to the older generation, with the younger one looking on, I would now reverse the procedure. From here on I am addressing the younger generation with the elders listening in. Because I have not hesitated to expose the foibles of the older generation, which has become more and more the target for bitter and often justified attacks from all sides, that by no means implies that one must say amen to all that the young say and do.

If the history of past student rebellions in Europe has anything to say concerning what is taking place in America at present, it is this: Beware that you are not led to masochistic extremes which may produce the opposite of what you seek. Instead of taking a step toward the solution of social and political problems, the suicidal, self-destructive tactics of the few may crush all hopes for betterment, bring to power the very reactionary forces you seek to conquer, and loose new terrors hitherto not thought possible. It was a student assassin's act that led to World War I, while "The bomb that killed Alexander II," observed Bernard Pares, the historian who witnessed the terrorism of Russian students, "put an end to the faint beginnings of Russian constitutionalism."[20]

Student protest, always a factor in institutions of higher learning, has in our time given way, to frightening eruptions of violence that have brought bloodshed to hundreds, terror to thousands, and closed down entire universities. Some of these tactics seem designed not so much to change as to destroy the university itself. This leads to the question of how different this direction-less destruction by students of the very institutions they seek to redeem is from the action of an American general who annihilates a South Vietnam village "in order to save it."

If student violence on campus is difficult to understand, the response of the universities to the violence has been utterly confusing. Whether because of guilt, sympathy, or inability to handle a challenge of such dimensions, administrators have capitulated for the most part to students demands. One of the most ludicrous examples of this to date was the action of the former president of

Cornell, Dr. James A. Perkins, who, confronted with armed Negro students, put the university airplane at the disposal of several militants who wanted to go to New York to purchase bongo drums—at a cost of $2,000 from university and student funds—for Malcolm X Memorial Day!

Addressing youthful extremism, Leo Rosten wrote a letter to an angry young man.

"You say your generation 'wants to be understood.' Well, so does mine. How much have you tried to understand others? You pillory us for injustices not of our making, frictions not of our choice, dilemmas that history (or our forbears or the sheer intractability of events) presented to us. You say we 'failed' because you face so many awful problems. Will you then accept blame for all the problems that exist (and they will) when you are twenty years older? And how do you know that all problems are soluble? Or soluble swiftly? Or soluble, given the never-infinite resources, brains and experience any generation is endowed with?

"I say that you are failing us— in failing to learn and respect discomforting facts; in failing to learn how to think (it is easier to complain); in using violence to shut down colleges; in shamefully denying the freedom of others to study and to teach; in barbarously slandering and abusing and shouting down those who disagree with you; in looting, stealing, and defiling; in failing to see how much more complicated social problems are than you blindly assume; in acting out of an ignorance for which idealism is no excuse, and a hysteria for which youth is no defense.

"You want to 'wreck this slow, inefficient democratic system.' It took the human race centuries of thought and pain and suffering and hard experiment to devise it. Democracy is not a 'state' but a process; it is a way of solving human problems, a way of hobbling power, a way of protecting every minority from the awful, fatal tyranny of either the few or the many. Whatever its imperfections, democracy is the only system man has discovered that makes possible change without violence. Do you really prefer bloodshed to debate? Quick dictates to slow law? This democracy made possible a great revolution in the past thirty-five years (a profound transfer of power, a distribution of wealth, an improvement of living and health) without 'liquidating' millions, without suppressing free speech, without the obscenities of dogma enforced by terror. This 'slow, inefficient' system protects people like me against people like you, and (though you don't realize it) protects innocents like you against those 'reactionary ... fascist forces' you fear; they, like you, prefer 'action to talk.' As for 'security'—at what price? The most 'secure' of human institutions is a prison; would you choose to live in one?"[2][1]

The problem becomes even more complex when we note that this period of destruction, bloodshed and violence on the campuses and in the cities has been followed by a dramatic silence. In recent months there have been a few strikes and marches, some memorial services at the universities to commemorate the tragic events of 1967-69, and a vast quiet. The conditions that first evoked student protest have not altered: the need for change remains as powerful as before. But the visible response has begun to change.

One example is the series of communes which have emerged across the country. Some are weird colonies given over to free sex and drugs. Others, however, are serious attempts to discover an answer to rampant materialism and egocentrism, to search out an alternative to our plastic, fragmentized, computerized society that might offer some measure of mutuality and continuity of existence. There is an increased interest in the authentic life-style of Israel's Kibbutzim, as evidenced by the rapid rise in the number of young American Jews now seriously inquiring into Israeli communes, particularly the religious ones.

Another impressive development is the surprising demand for increased Jewish education on the college campuses. One consequence of this surge is that, while an overabundance of Ph.D.'s is presently flooding the academic market, there is a marked shortage of those who have advanced degrees in Jewish studies and are qualified to teach on the university level. This growing demand for Jewish education is more than a desire to join the race for ethnic recognition. It is, in some measure, a protest against the hyprocisy of pride and ignorance, and a reaching out for the wholeness of self. One discovers a turning toward the mystical and a new openness to Hassidic Judaism, not only to the beauty of its teachings but to the living experience of its songs, its prayers and its community. Applications for entrance into rabbinical seminaries have multiplied, as have the number of seminaries themselves, some of which are innovative in their approach.

The remarkable emergence of a new generation of Russian Jews, which rejects its parents' blind, non-critical pattern of assimilation for a proud affirmation of Jewishness and a feverish search for identity—sometimes at the peril of their lives—has struck a deep responsive chord among the new generation of American Jews, many of whom have made the cause of Russian Jewry their own. The new phenomenon of independent Jewish student newspapers—several of which are as good as anything the American-Jewish press has to offer—has grown to more than 35 with a readership of some 350,000, affording a vehicle of expression and debate for the young in their own idiom on the broadest Jewish issues. Jewish graduates of professional schools show an increased interest in being placed in social agencies or at least in being permitted to devote a portion of their time to community concerns, in contrast to the singleminded search in the past for a job with an established firm. Nor is youth alone in their quest. Women have joined hands in a liberation movement that seeks similar goals of self-knowledge and responsibility to society.

Such revolution implies two equally important acts: a tearing down and a building up, the latter far more difficult than the former. The Jews' rejection of the status quo has always been in the name of the kind of society they would like to build. They must say "no" to what is because they have already said "yes" to what ought to be. The greatest revolutionaries in all of human history were Israel's prophets. When Jeremiah was called by God to go out to a corrupt society and change it, the command contained two injunctions: he was told

"to root out and to pull down."
and
"to build and to plant."[22]

Only when both are joined together do we have true revolution. The trouble with the radicalism of many young people today is that it only goes half way; it is just not radical enough.

It is instructive to examine the survey which was printed in the Israeli paper, *Maariv*, of reactions of Israeli university students to student revolts in other parts of the world.

"We don't believe in anarchic revolt just to be against something. If we want to oppose, then we should be ready to come up with better ideas and challenge the establishment with a superior ideology . . . Revolution is not always necessary progress. We can be dynamic without throwing paving stones at the police. Maybe some students seek action to prove they are virile. Those of us who have been in the Israeli army have seen action and don't have to prove anything—to ourselves or to others . . . Students rise up against a rigid Establishment. But ours, with all its faults, is itself a revolutionary Establishment. We see much to improve, but certainly not to overthrow or destroy . . . To leaders of student revolt in all countries, especially if they are Jewish, we say: If you feel you want to help build a new world, or want to throw off the yoke of middle class conventionalism—we welcome you to Israel."[2][3]

Some readers will be astonished at the claim that Judaism is a radical revolution. As they see it expressed in their own community by way of dull Friday evening services, shul politics, middle class morality, Sisterhood fashion shows, the Center steam room, the Club golf course and bar, and the perennial fund raising, Judaism is anything but radical or revolutionary. Banal and pagan might be better descriptions. The tragic truth is that authentic Judaism cannot be judged by what Jews, the Jewish community, or even—to our shame—what some synagogues are doing these days. To do so would be to err. As quoted earlier, Abraham Heschel rightly claims that "Judaism is the least known religion." Least known, he means, not only to gentiles but to the Jews themselves; even, one might add, to many of those more "active" in Jewish affairs. Who can deny that with Herculean effort we have succeeded in turning the miraculous into the commonplace and in telescoping the exceptional into the ordinary, while keeping the real grandeur under wraps?

The time has come to expose the truth. For many it is too late. They are too fixed in their habits to change. The younger generation, however, has not as yet made up its mind. If we want to win a part of them for Judaism, we must show them the radical and revolutionary nature of the faith into which they have been born. It is not enough any more to point nostalgically to the past or to ship the young off to Camp Ramah and their parents to Israel in order that they catch the feeling of Jewish authenticity. Such escapes into time and space are no longer adequate. Our own lives, communally and individually, must begin to reflect the seriousness and the splendor of that authenticity here and now.

Let us inquire into Jewish authenticity by contrasting three remarkably revolutionary verses in the Bible with their contemporary counterparts.

1.

Personal Life

Using drugs is one of the favorite and most infamous recourses of today's radical youth. Once you "turn on," colors glow, sensations are heightened, the mind expands enormously, and one begins to hear the languages of new worlds.

But is "turning on" radical? After all, what does it require of us? To inhale smoke, swallow a pill, or puncture the skin with a needle? It is all quite simple, quite automatic, just the introduction of a foreign chemical which induces changes in the body, so easily do we turn ourselves into human guinea pigs in a home-made laboratory. Nor do the immediate sensations remain. They must be restimulated. And with each restimulation, a craving for higher doses and more powerful stimulants results.

Drugs are neither very radical nor very revolutionary. They are, and always have been, an escape route from the disappointments and the opportunities, the despair and the challenge, the tragedies and the glories of life itself.

The most radical statement about personal life ever uttered is found in the Bible:

"Kedoshim tihyu ki kadosh Ani Adonoy Elohaykhem."

"Ye shall be holy, for I, the Lord your God, am holy."[24]

Let us examine this command.

At first glance, it seems absurd. Is it possible for man to be holy? And to be holy because God is holy? Are they not opposites? Man is man, and God is God. Man can be an animal in this world, seeking after pleasure and power, or he can be an angel in the next world, basking in the rays of the *Shechinah*. But holy here and now? Never! Impossible for flesh and blood! How can this frail creature, this vessel of passions and whims, of folly, vanity, and foolishness, capable of error and evil, become holy? God, of course, is holy. But does it follow that if God, who is perfect in all His ways, is holy, then man, who is a mass of imperfections, be unholy?

Yet the opposite is the claim of Scripture. God says to us, "Thou shalt be holy"—that is, you have it in your power to be holy—"*because I am holy.*"[25] True, God seems to be saying, you are an animal, but an animal with a soul who can thereby transcend himself. I Who am holy made you. I put something of Myself into you. You can ignore that part of Me which is in you and become a beast, or, if you want to, you can develop it and become what you were meant to become, My image on earth. Become holy. This is your task as man. Become *humanly* holy, with all your impulses and yearnings. You have the power to do so, because I, Who made you, will help you do it. "Sin coucheth at the door, but you may rule over it."[26] ". . . I have set before you life and death, the blessing and the curse; therefore choose life . . . "[27]

The holiness command is a radical command; it touches our very roots. It is revolutionary because it demands utter and permanent transformation.

How can man be holy?

This is a perennial question. The answers given are usually variations on a single theme: annihilate your desires, crush your impulses, escape from the world. Judaism has never taken that unnatural tack. To it, human impulses are neutral and not evil. It is man's use of them that makes them good or evil. To be holy, man must take hold of his life precisely as it is, striving to sublimate his energies to higher purposes through a series of mitzvot in the service of God. Thus, for example, the mitzvah of *kashrut* sublimates the act of eating; marriage, the sexual appetite; and the Sabbath and *tsedakah*, the acquisitive instinct. The raging desires of man are transformed and ennobled into lofty impulses. If the way to produce metal is by refining crude ore, eliminating the slag, and permitting the pure product to emerge, so it is with man. "Why were the mitzvot given?" asks the Midrash. The answer: "in order to refine [purify] man."[28] Man, in his original state, is a mass of conflicting desires, capable of good or evil, a terrible-wonderful creature. Through the discipline of the mitzvot, the divine potential hidden within each man is gradually released, and man rises to the stature he was created for: "but little lower than the angels."[29]

A group of Hasidim, debating over whose *rebbe* was supreme, began relating wonder stories about their respective masters. One, it was told, could "see" what was happening in the next village, another could "predict" what would happen in the future, and a third could "cure" the sick and lame. Finally a Hasid who until then had been silent said, "My *rebbe* can perform a greater miracle than any you have mentioned." "What is that?" they asked. "He is able to make a Jew!"

Is that not, in fact, the most difficult and wonderful of all miracles? To allow the light that is within us to illumine, then conquer, the dark side of life; to fashion out of man a creature sensitive, disciplined, responsive, charitable, and kind. That is indeed a miracle. It does not come of itself by signing one's name, taking an oath, swallowing a pill, or plunging a hypodermic needle into one's arm.

The last Olympics took place with great fanfare and much record-breaking. As millions admired the hundreds of strong, swift bodies on television sets the world over, many must have wondered how ordinary men are turned into athletes with such wonderful control of their bodies that they are able to accomplish the most difficult feats with ease. It is achieved, we all know, through a rigid schedule of training, which gradually provides a marvelous coordination of their bodies whose latent physical powers are developed to their fullest. It is the result of constant discipline. Athletes will deny themselves food, drink, and cigarettes, devote hours each day to strenuous exercise, and even rise at five or six in the morning to swim for two hours before classes. The regimen required of the musician is, if anything, more demanding, because it does not cease at the age of thirty or so, as with the athlete, but remains throughout life. No artist performs without exacting and exhausting practice. The pianist, probably from earliest childhood, devotes hour upon hour every day to a rigid schedule that is meant to draw forth all the concealed, hidden talent until finally a trained musician emerges.

What is so easily understood in regard to physical or musical skill is rarely applied to a far more important part of life, the moral aspect. Here sloppiness is tolerated. Untold hours are invested in training not only physical and artistic skills, but intellectual ones as well: mathematics, languages, sciences, the whole spectrum of academic disciplines. But what preparation, practice, or discipline do we devote to moral living? It is here that Judaism speaks to us.

It has long been understood that the human condition

requires, above all, moral training. Judaism urges upon us a rigid schedule of discipline through the mitzvot, every day of the year, from birth to death, in the knowledge that man's spiritual potential must be developed like his physical and aesthetic potential. There is a major difference, however. While most of us do not become athletes or musicians, all of us have the capacity to be human beings in whom moral values are paramount.

We tend to think of the *Shulhan Arukh*, the classic compendium of Jewish law, as an old-fashioned book of little help to us today. But upon opening it one is struck by the power and the rightness of the very first passage:

"Rise up in the morning like a lion to serve thy Creator."

With these words it initiates man into another day of work and worry. How typical of the Jewish spirit! As soon as the bands of sleep fall from one's eyes and before foreign thoughts can arouse temptation, one is bidden to gather all one's strength in order to break the bonds of sloth and selfishness to begin what must be the central concern of all—the service of God.

When should man be holy?

Is holiness, in other words, restricted to certain places or times—on the Sabbath, on Yom Kippur, while in the synagogue at prayer, during the study of the Torah? Of course, one ought to be holy then. But not only then. One can be holy in any place, and at any time. The sages point out that if we are commanded to fast on the tenth of Tishri (Yom Kippur), we are commanded to eat on the ninth, and that as much holiness may invest the one act as the other. Indeed, a higher level of holiness may be achieved through eating than fasting, because it is more difficult. It depends on how we eat. The time or place does not determine holiness. One can be holy when talking, if his words are pure and true, or when doing business, if his actions are upright.

"Judaism," writes Martin Buber, "can be summed up in a single sentence: God can be beheld in each thing and reached through each pure deed. In the Hasidic teaching, the whole world is only a word out of the mouth of God. Nonetheless, the least thing in the world is worthy that through it God should reveal Himself to the man who truly seeks Him; for no thing can exist without a divine spark, and each person can uncover and redeem this spark at each time and through each action, even the most ordinary, if only he performs it in purity, wholly directed to God and concentrated in Him. Therefore, it will not do to serve God only in isolated hours and with set words and gestures. One must serve God with one's whole life, with the whole of the everyday, with the whole of reality. The salvation of man does not lie in his holding himself far removed from the worldly, but in consecrating it to holy, to divine meaning; his work and his food, his rest and his wandering, the structure of the family and the structure of society. It lies in his preserving the great love of God for all creatures, yes, for all things. Hasidism took the social form of a great popular community—not an order of the secluded, not a brotherhood of the select, but a popular community in all its medley, in all its spiritual and social multiplicity. Never yet in Europe has such a community thus established the whole of life as a unity on the basis of the inwardly known. Here is no separation between faith and work, between truth and verification, or, in the language of today, between morality and politics; here all is one kingdom, one spirit, one reality."[30]

And who is holy?

Only the priest of ancient times, the saint, the miracle-worker, the rabbi? No. The words are, "Kedoshim tihyu"—"You (that is, all of you) shall be holy." Again and again Moses is told to "Speak unto *the whole people* of Israel. They are to be a kingdom of priests and a holy people."[31] No one is to be excluded. No one is exempt from the holiness commandment: not the pauper or the millionaire, the student or the teacher, the salesman or the manufacturer, the patient or the doctor.

What a remarkable claim! There is no one sacrosanct way to God which all men must follow, but each man's way—as father, merchant, or teacher—can become a holy way. It is not so much *what* we do that matters, but *how* we do it. We were not destined to be a people who so feared the world that its elite would renounce it for God, as monks or nuns do, while the rest were condemned to marriage, which Paul understood as a concession to human sinfulness.[32] Rather every member of the people Israel was expected to be a priest within the world, within his own home. In Judaism, the common man does not relegate to the select few a special spiritual status to perform sacraments on his behalf because he is unworthy and sinful. Judaism teaches that every man is a child of God. Every man is called to become what his nature permits him to become. Every man, on his own rung of human existence, in his own peculiar situation, is expected to make of his life a service of God by doing the mitzvot and by hallowing the profane. In this way, each man can achieve the miraculous, each man can be holy.

Out of this belief was born the wonderful concept of the *baal habayit*, which literally means the "master of the house" but more correctly, the "father-priest." For each home in Israel was to be a *mikdash m'at*, a miniature sanctuary. Thus when the father, who an hour earlier might have been immersed in his daily work, enters his home on a Sabbath Eve and lifts the *kiddush* cup, he is no longer a salesman or a merchant or even just a husband, but the priest of an ancient people whose table has become an altar, his home a sanctuary, and his family the actors in an age-old drama in which the hallowing power of God and man reaches into the not-yet-hallowed.

"We live in a generation which has rebelled against the father... The revolution of the sons is a rebellion against hypocrisy... Revolutions, like wars, are often tragically inevitable. But one thing the rebellious generations will have to learn: that is, to be a father... In the end all the sons' complaints become senseless, if the son does not learn to take over the duties of the father... The *baal habayit* is the father who knows his duty, which consists in creating a holy sanctuary at home, where good is done and where this is not hypocrisy, but genuine goodness..."

"The intellectual" regards himself "as the embodiment of prophetic religion in his criticism of society, in his fight for the socially and economically oppressed." But is "there no justification in the Bible for the head of the family, the father who simply and humbly [bears] the daily burden?... This man is not an intellectual... but he leads an intellectual life by constantly linking his everyday life with God. He works, and with his earnings he supports himself and his family. The table in his home is an altar at which prayers are said, and in the peace of his home his wife, his children and himself discover that a house, a human dwelling-place, can be like a House of God. A human home, like a house of prayer, can achieve holiness. A dwelling-house, the small place where people eat, sleep, work and rest, becomes a sanctuary because of the *baal habayit*."[33]

If you seek radicalism regarding personal life, then it can be found in the holiness Commandment—*kedoshim tihyu*—which seeks to bring about the ultimate miracle—a holy man, a holy community, and a holy people.

2.

Economic Life

If hippies think that "turning on" is a radical mode of living one's personal life, the Communists might claim that "Workers of the world, unite!" is the most revolutionary formula regarding economic life. To be sure, the collective awareness that Communism awakened in the hearts of the dispossessed and the changes that were subsequently brought about by their action have produced many blessings. But who would deny that at least as noteworthy have been the curses of Communism: its savage cruelty, its reign of terror, its ruthless disregard of human dignity. The Communist program is not radical enough.

A much more revolutionary statement pertaining to economics is found in the Bible and can be summed up in two Hebrew words spoken by God:

"*Li ha'aretz*"—"The earth is Mine."[3 4]

This too appears to be an absurd statement. How ridiculous to assert that the world belongs to God. The two reigning theories of property—capitalism and socialism—claim the opposite, that everything belongs, individually or collectively, not to God, but to man. Capitalism asserts that property is the province of the individual, and most of our institutions, laws, courts, jails, and police, exist primarily to protect man's property. To be sure, capitalism was a great advance over the prevailing feudal system which it superseded, when most people were serfs belonging to the local prince who could do what he willed with their possessions. But what may have begun as an improvement over the past, in time developed its own weaknesses, with the gradual movement of more and more wealth into fewer and fewer hands. The injustices engendered by this system led directly to the creation of a new theory of property—socialism—which sought to solve the problem of the haves and have-nots in one sweeping reform: the transferral of all property from the individual to the state. That sounded good, at first. But who is "the state"? Those who have power, the oligarchy that rules, the dictator?

Contrary to both these views is the Biblical theory of economics, the central principle of which is that God owns the world! He created it. It belongs to Him. But he lets us use it. That is the key—*He lets us use it*. We are only his stewards, using the world under the conditions of the moral law which He has established in our lives, just as He has implanted the laws of nature in the physical universe. Woe to the man who violates either! If we live justly, the blessing of the earth we use is ours; if not we shall inherit misery. Or, to use the language of the Bible, "the land will vomit out its inhabitants."[35] If we choose evil too long, we may succeed in destroying the earth and ourselves as well in one great mushroom cloud. Atomic weapons have enabled us to understand in scientific terms the Biblical insistence on a moral law upon which the earth itself depends.

Biblical economics were not limited to a solemn statement of principle but were boldly implemented in a series of concrete laws, for it is one thing to enunciate a vague theory and quite another to reduce it to daily precept. Although some of these laws have since been discarded as utopian, others persist. And all of the laws, whether or not in current usage, may serve us in varying degrees as a guide for immediate action, a goal to strive for, and a standard by which we can judge ourselves from time to time.

Let us examine three such laws.

The first of these laws is the Sabbath, the command that every seventh day we cease our work. Why? Because in working we learn to bend nature to our will and begin to believe that we are the master and the world is ours to do with as we see fit. Therefore, we are bidden to withdraw, one day a week, from our conquest of the world in order to remember that God is the Creator, and man but His creature.

The second law extends the idea of the Sabbath from one day a week to one year in seven. "When ye come into the land which I gave you, then shall the land keep a sabbath unto the Lord. Six years thou shalt sow thy field, and six years thou shalt prune thy vineyard . . . But in the seventh year shall be a sabbath of solemn rest for the land, a sabbath unto the Lord."[36] The "land" is to keep a sabbath to help man understand that his ownership is not absolute and to enable man to nurture his mind and spirit during that year. This was the original sabbatical year.

But the third and most radical of these laws, also a multiple of seven, is the Jubilee year. "You shall count seven weeks of years, so that you have a total of 49 years, and in the seventh month, on the tenth day of the month, on the day of atonement, you shall blow the shofar throughout your land, and you shall hallow the fiftieth year. And it shall be a jubilee for you, and each of you shall return to his land. Do not wrong one another, but fear your God, for I, the Lord, am your God."[37]

When the people of Israel entered the Promised Land, it was divided among the twelve tribes and then equally among all the families belonging to each tribe. For fifty years a free and open commerce reigned, some becoming rich and others poor, the land changing hands accordingly. But when fifty years had passed and the jubilee shofar was sounded, all such land was redistributed equally as at first.

What the jubilee law does is to prevent one from selling ownership in the land, because one has no right to do so. The land belongs to God. One may only lease it for a number of years—let us say twenty—until the next Jubilee year. Thus in every generation, children enjoyed the same advantage of a fair start as their father had before them. Transposing this system to modern society, it would be equivalent to pooling, every fifty years, all our individual accumulated wealth—our cash, stocks, property, etc.—in one vast treasury and then redistributing it equally among all the citizens.

The poet Heine said that this is not the abolition of property but rather the moralization of property. And the economist, Henry George, explained: "It is not the protection of property but the protection of humanity that is the aim of the Mosaic code. Its sabbath day and sabbath year secure even to the lowliest, rest and leisure. With the blast of the jubilee trumpet, the redivision of the land secures again to the poorest his fair share in the bounty of the common Creator."[38]

I know of no economic radicalism which can duplicate these laws or the principle on which they are based. True, the jubilee law in all probability was not observed for many centuries, but the notion that we do not own our property has never left the Jewish people. It is the thought that what we have really belongs to God, and is given to us only that we might deal justly with it, that is responsible, in large measure, for Israel's unique concept of charity. Contrary to the accepted Christian notion of charity as pity or mercy—something beyond the call of duty—the Hebrew word for charity—*tsedakah*—means, not mercy, but justice or righteousness—that which it is man's duty to do.

The Jewish concept of charity as justice is captured in

this story. A *shnorrer* used to go to the house of a rich Jew in Poland to get a hand-out each week. One day he knocked on the door and asked, "Could I have my money?" to which the rich man replied, "I'm sorry, this week we will have to let it go. You see, I got a fur coat for my wife, and we are planning a long visit to Baden Baden." Scowling, the shnorrer replied, "What do you mean, you're planning a trip to the spa in Baden Baden and you bought your wife a fur coat—on *my* money?"

Such a tale emerges only out of Jewish folklore. It is not to be found among the Irish or Scottish or any other peoples' tales. Why? Because the Biblical Talmudic notion that the earth is the Lord's and man only His trustee became uniquely fixed in the Jewish psyche through centuries of teaching and living. This, by the way, is the whole idea of the Jewish National Fund, which only rents but never sells land. It is the idea behind the kibbutz movement, too. In fact, it is the motivating force behind the whole Zionist experiment which claims that the land of Israel is not meant to be just another state, but rather a bold venture into the fulfillment of the prophets' passion for justice in the daily life of man.

There is a great dream embedded in the Jews' belief that God owns the world. Perhaps it is more than a little responsible for the large number of social idealists and economic revolutionaries that the Jews have produced all through history. Real economic radicalism, then, is to turn the world back to God through the service of man.

3.

Political Life

We have dealt with radical conceptions of personal life and economics. What about world politics? The Nazis proclaimed a doctrine of "Blood and Soil," that would lead to "Germany today—Tomorrow the World!" in the belief that they were the political revolutionaries of their time. These were not very radical ideas. Others had proclaimed them, and forgotten them, long ago.

The most radical statement ever uttered regarding world politics we may never have recognized as being related to politics at all. It is:

"Hear O Israel, the Lord our God, the Lord is One!"

This is ultimately a political statement, because it proclaims that truth which alone makes possible the hope of one political world, namely, the underlying spiritual unity which draws all men together.

This, too, seems absurd. Unity in our world? Oneness in this fragmented universe, where people barely converse with one another; where languages, customs, hatreds, and alliances form barriers to divide us? The Iron Curtain has never been more tightly drawn than today. Fifty years ago, one could travel to many lands without so much as a passport. Today Africa, Asia, South America, Eastern and Western Europe are worlds unto themselves. It seems all the more strange that the Jew could utter this proclamation of unity at a time when he did not even know what was at the other end of the Mediterranean Sea or beyond the Tigris and Euphrates Rivers, when he was ignorant of most foreign tongues, and when he had no television to view distant places or jets to visit them. Yet he *knew* that the world was one. He knew because he believed that God was One and that the One God had put the potential for oneness in the world by breathing something of His spirit into every human creature. According to Biblical legend, when God created the world, He did it by making a single man first, so that all men in future generations could say, "We are all children of one father, all brothers."

When a pious Jew who truly understands the *Shema* recites it, his mind dwells upon the last word, "one," and he stretches out the last letter— *Ehad-d-d-d.* What is in his mind when he does this? Three things.

First, he remembers that in the beginning there was unity throughout the universe. God was One in Himself, because He was One with the world. And God was at One with the world because man was at one with his fellow man. And man was at one with his fellow man because he was at one with himself. Peace reigned; justice prevailed; and it was good in the sight of God.

Second, he is aware that that oneness has been shattered, and that the world, mankind, and each individual is fragmented. It is this alienation from our true source which explains the tension between what we ought to do and what we want to do, the struggle between the "evil urge" and the "good urge" which dwell side by side in each heart and which tears us apart a hundred times a day. It is not so much that we do not know what is right, but that we persist in choosing what is wrong. That is man's tragic flaw. Furthermore, there is division not only within man, but between man and his brother—competition, enmity, hatred. We are tempted to outdo our neighbors, envy their successes, and rejoice in their failures. Men tend to regard each other not as neighbors or brothers, but as individuals to be manipulated for one's own benefit. It is these divisions among and within men that divide God from the world. Indeed, they drive God out of the world. God is in exile.

The third thought in the mind of the Jew when he says the *Shema* is that he believes that God, no longer at one with a fragmented world, is striving to join Himself to it, and that he must devote his life to the realization of that reunited world. How can man help to bring God out of exile and back to the world? First, by binding up the tattered fragments of his own soul so that he becomes a whole person again, and then, by making his relationship with his neighbor one of love, understanding, and friendship. This is the Messianic hope: that the human creature who remembers the former unity and sees the present fragmentation will work toward a future wholeness, when God will be One with all mankind because all mankind will be one with itself.

Each day the Jew dwells on this vision when he recites the *Alenu* prayer.

"We hope for the day
When the world will be perfected
Under the Kingdom of the Almighty,
And all mankind will call upon Thy Name,
And that Thou wilt turn unto Thyself
All the wicked of the earth.
For the Kingdom, is Thine,
And to all eternity
Thou wilt reign in glory.
As it is written in Thy Torah:
The Lord shall reign forever and ever.
And it has been foretold:
The Lord shall be King over all the earth.
On that day
The Lord shall be One,
And His name One."

4.

The Underground

We Jews have been accused of plotting to overthrow the world. A vicious anti-Semite of the last century wrote a scurrilous pamphlet called *The Protocols of the Elders of Zion*. Its foul slander, which accused the Jews of infiltrating every major city on every continent to gather in secret meetings and to scheme how to rule the world, has brought and still brings untold misery upon the people of Israel. The Czarists, the Fascists, and the Nazis have used it to justify their persecution of the Jews. The Communists and the Arabs still use it. With the emergence of each new group of racists, these lies are spewed forth again and again. Jews have learned to hate that document for the misery it has caused millions of our people.

And yet, in that very slander is a kernel of truth.

The truth is that we are scattered throughout the world, that we are a radical underground, that we do have secret meetings—they take place each morning and evening in every synagogue in the world—and that those meetings are indeed a plot to overthrow the world.

But that is as far as the parallel goes.

For our conspiracy is not that *we* should rule. Our prayers—and our lives—are for a world liberated from tyranny and misery that *God* might rule. For centuries this has been the secret "plot" of every Jew, from Abraham to Moses to Isaiah to Rashi to the Baal Shem to Rav Kook to every Jewish child who learns the *alef-bet*. Wherever the Jew has lived, from Jerusalem to Alexandria to Rome to Lisbon to Frankfurt to Prague to Vilna to Warsaw to New York to Moscow and back to Jerusalem once again, he has dreamed, planned, and worked for such a time. He has done so because there have been indelibly inscribed upon the soul of his people those three ancient Scriptural affirmations:

That man can be holy.

That he can create a just society.

That God will one day be reunited with His creation.

Young people claim they want to revolt because they can no longer bear the immorality of our society. They should revolt. It is time to become intolerant of corruption.

But many of the young are not radical enough. They concentrate on tearing down, without having a vision of what they want to build.

That is too easy, and too dangerous.

If our youth want to revolt, let them do so—as Jews. Authentic Jews are commanded to wage a daily war against evil. And if the young are alienated from the Jewish community, so are many rabbis, teachers, and leaders. If we want to say *NO* to what exists today, then let us say *YES* to what ought to be. If we say no to the Establishment, then let us speak:

in the name of Holiness,

in the name of Justice,

and, in the name of God.

Let the total redemption of mankind be the goal.

Let the words of the prophets kindle a fire in all our hearts until "justice wells up as water",[39] until "swords are beaten into ploughshares,"[40] and until the Torah "is written in our hearts."[41]

Revolt? Yes! Let us revolt, young and old alike. For we have been born into the most revolutionary people that ever lived. It is the Children of Israel, throughout the ages, who have been the true revolutionaries, the people who have fought every tyrant in history, who have kept burning the candles of justice, peace, and hope in the darkest times, and who still today, in Moscow, New York, Jerusalem, and all over the world, carry the unborn Messiah in their souls for a future day to come.

That is God's word to Israel, according to the prophet:
"I have put My words in thy mouth
And covered thee in the shadow of My hand
That I might plant the heavens
And lay the foundations of the Earth."[42]

NOTES

[1] George Kennan, Address to International Association for Cultural Freedom Conference, Princeton, New Jersey, December 2, 1968; reprinted in *The New York Times*, December 4, 1968.

[2] Lewis S. Feuer, *The Conflict of Generations* (New York: Basic Books Inc., 1969), p. 10.

[3] John D. Rockefeller II, "In Praise of Young Revolutionaries," *Saturday Review*, December 14, 1968, pp. 18-19.

[4] James Michener, "Revolution in Middle Class Values," *New York Times Magazine*, August 18, 1968, pp. 20-21.

[5] Alvin Schorr, *Explorations in Social Policy* (New York: Basic Books Inc., 1968).

[6] Judge Charles Wyzansky, Jr., "A Federal Judge Digs the Young," *Saturday Review*, July 20, 1968. p. 15.

[7] Amitai Etzioni, "Campus Ferment—Search for New Values," *Hadassah Magazine*, May, 1969, p. 10.

[8] Dr. Calvin Plimpton, letter to President Nixon, April 29, 1969.

[9] Roderick MacLeish, "Revolt on Campus," *Readers Digest*, June, 1969, p. 71.

[10] Samuel H. Dresner, *God, Man and Atomic War* (New York: Living Books, Inc., 1966), pp. 22-23.

[11] John Wharton, "Toward an Affirmative Morality," *Saturday Review*, July 12, 1969, p. 11.

[12] H. Schwartz, ed., *Jewish College Youth Speak Their Minds* (New York: American Jewish Committee, 1969), pp. 19, 25.

[13] Sylvia Rothschild, "In Defense of the Jewish Mother," *Council Woman*, Winter 1969, p. 8.

[14] Abraham Heschel, *The Earth is the Lord's* (New York: Abelard-Schuman Ltd., 1950), p. 107.

[15] Abraham Heschel, *The Insecurity of Freedom* (New York: Farrar, Straus & Giroux, 1966), p. 191.

[16] *The New York Times*, May 21, 1966.

[17] Jerome R. Mintz, *Legends of the Hasidim* (Chicago: University of Chicago Press, 1968), pp. 60-61.

[18] Lincoln Steffens, *Autobiography of Lincoln Steffens* (New York: The Literary Guild, 1931); quoted in *The Golden Land*, Azriel Eisenberg, ed. (New York: Yoseloff, 1964), pp. 207-8.

[19] Rothschild, p. 8.

[20] Bernard Pares, *A History of Russia* (New York: Alfred A. Knopf, 1953).

[21] Leo Rosten, "A Letter to an Angry Young Man," *Look*, November 12, 1968, p. 28.

[22] Jer. 1:10.

[23] Reprinted in *Boston Jewish Advocate*, September 5, 1968.

[24] Lev. 19:2.

[25] *Ibid*.

[26] Gen. 4:7.

[27] Deut. 30:19.

[28] Midrash Beraishit Rabbah 44:1.

[29] Ps. 8:6.

[30] Martin Buber, *Hasidism and Modern Man* (New York: Horizon Press, 1958), p. 49.

[31] Exod. 19:6.

[32] 1 Cor. 7:1-9.

[33] Ignaz Maybaum, *The Jewish Home* (London: James Clarke, 1945), pp. 20-21; 27-28.

[34] Lev. 25:23.

[35] Lev. 18:25.

[36] Lev. 25:2-4.

[37] Lev. 25:8-10, 17.

[38] J. H. Hertz, *Pentateuch and Haftorahs* (London: Soncino Press, 1968), pp. 532-33, Lev. 25:10.

[39] Amos 5:24.

[40] Isa. 2:4.

[41] Jer. 31:33.

[42] Isa. 51:16.